Lullaby for One Fist

Lullaby for One Fist

Andrea Werblin

Wesleyan University Press

Middletown, Connecticut

Published by Wesleyan University Press, Middletown, CT 06459
© 2001 by Andrea Werblin
Printed in the United States of America
5 4 3 2 1

Library of Congress Cataloging-in-Publication Data

Werblin, Andrea
Lullaby for one fist / by Andrea Werblin
    p. cm.
ISBN 0–8195–6462–1 (cloth : alk. paper) — ISBN 0–8195–6463–X (paper : alk.
paper)
I. Title.
PS3573.E6 L85 2001
811'.6—dc21   00–012380

Grateful acknowledgement is made to the editors of the magazines in which
some of the poems in this volume first appeared. "Lovestruck" and "Who Sees
As Whole Must First Be Us" first appeared in *Alligator Juniper,* Fall 1997. "Not
Knowing" first appeared in *SUN DOG: The Southeast Review* 12, no. 2, 1992.
"Saints in the Hedges" first appeared in *Willow Springs* 40, June 1997.

for mom, dad, and lisa

Contents

contents

three

acknowledgments

Many thanks to many teachers: Jane Miller, Steve Orlen, James Tate, Debra Gregerman, Priscilla Becker, Laura Newbern, Vinnie Scorziello, Victoria Richardson Warneck, Terry Vaughn, Enza Vescera, Jenny Edwards, Fatima Muniain, Kendra Gaines, Paul Charette, and the city of Barcelona, Spain.

For inherited eccentricities and unconditional love, I thank the Labins family, especially Stephen, Lois, Judy, Chuck, Annie, and Ruth Helene Alexander.

I am grateful to Bridget David Macleod for her optimism, honesty, and best-ever sense of humor.

Special thanks to Suzanna Tamminen.

Lullaby for One Fist

Barrio with Sketchy Detail

Except for the chickens humming to each other,
making themselves look boneless in the dirt,
I want no memory of this place.

I will leave gingerly.
I will leave strung out.
I will leave rocking on my heels in unbearable heat,

the Mexican girls still faking and mourning Selena
from their perfect cement stoops,
not yet sworn to the anger hanging
from their papas' mouths like cigarettes.

I will leave stunned, from across the room.
I will leave by instinct, my tongue intact.
I will leave understanding it

was always coming, before that night, even
before we met. Marta will stand quiet, a glyph,
Pedro offer beer in cups. We'll sit.

When I leave, the sky will be a gouache of scratches,
the morning sluggish, a cactus flowering.
Or I will leave in blistered dark. It will still be true.

one

Lovestruck

First it's a party that winks and blurts.
Then you agree to his idea of beauty.
Now you know the desire
to flinch for someone: gulping stomach,
the dumbstruck mouth a wound
to dive into, hope as the stalled horse
you heave against, tow.

Then it's his amatory tyrant
to your quizzical sidestep,
your zero-defect campaign
for him back vs. the elegiac
torpor reruns. A blow delivered
so wondrously you mistake it
for sanctuary, absurdity, fault.

Then, *chin-chin!* to the eye pillow filled
with lavender and flax. Even as you
grind your teeth you are thinking how
to make it better. The bed sheets shiver
on top of you, heartbeats. You're tired
as your suitcase. Small silences are still
the hardest to come by.

Let No One Put Asunder

Leonard hands off marriage
like a football to his son,
dances the Horah,
and takes a smoke.
My Chagall bra droops
in front to say, look,
is it really all this intimate?

I twist syllogisms to the swishy sound
of Lupita's dress. (If all emotion is
terror, and terror doesn't happen . . .)
To your logic I say: whatever, I'm lonely.

I promise you the dreamy blurred goats
are proof of faith; you can smash
the sky above them and still come out lovely.
It's a kind of commitment to the hook-and-eye thing,
a souvenir that aches and vows.

I keep hiking up this bra, my bottom line.
The red angel rushes me: *marry the beast.*

—after *Midsummer Night's Dream* (Chagall)

Lullaby for One Fist

As one survives the simple monsoon gone orange
so do the obedient palms swing calm in the static,
their litany of *no* gone away now.

Whoever taught us to keep going back
and back to garbled evenings, couches
rotting in back yards, now lives off the fat
of her words, a cat in her lap in New York state.

One never means to ask, *did his fist bloom*
as it graced through the car window to cup
her face? She nimbly buttoned her sweater,
protected her bleating chest.

If he tells her to please leave the room
because he thinks he might hit her,
is that abuse, physically speaking?

She says, *it was a holiday. Beer was involved.*
Dust had built up like a twister around the table legs.

Whoever gifted us as critics of our own time
badly spent, as ill-starred, too open,
is she home at last?

The barren corners have quit their verdicts
and weeds rise as testament to mowers.
She can't see that she can leave now.
Not all trees lean like over-wined kings.

A Letter From Stacey, So Close to God

This morning's a crash course in the *not now, please*
of less ill-designed Sundays, a ballfield of sulk—
You should know there are other kinds of wisdom to be wise to.
That voice you do cartwheels for is laughing,
sometimes—*you are not enough.*

All the morningbike assholes and kissed-lip mouths
of pre-teens ascending subway stares
get older and older, go lashless, self-helpful.
They telegraph their mistakes to you before they make them.

Behind the Dolphin café, behind the fish trash,
you are transported only by a thin cartoon
of the bass player's last-night bad shirt,
are made grander simply walking down
the center of your street, a video at 2 a.m.

Not enough, which got said to the face of your hand,
to your uneaten dumplings, your lack of grace.
Got said to the floppy stomach in the trawling
of bars and of psyches: *not enough.*
Smallest monster you had ever seen.

Habit of Wishing

For the sake of the scarecrow
dumbing his arms down
to make a point, please
continue sleeping in the field.
Go on making gestures too small
to write down or change.
Straw in your hair, a flat brightness
some mornings give your face,
and still—it's hard not to think
of this time as something neither
you nor the dullard wind
want to do.

These unfortunate weeks
I've sewn myself
a cruelly buttoned dress.
You'd need your bare teeth
to get it loose, which I call
"safety," null and useless.

Shambling eggshell days. Jealousy that contains
itself in the wood bowl meant for fruit.

There must be some new story
of leaving, where your sultry face means
little to prospective suitors, and I can
swallow my bath water with consequence,
not knowing the pulsing porch light
from the conceding heart, bruised.

Practicing for Real

A body can only be jealous
in two places and then
something gets more important
than the individual mood.

He left for work and I managed goodbye,
my own mind crunching on that slow day,
like a climate I could run from
and to—

entangled in those two places
a body could be, but, where
were they, for one, and,
possible exit, is that two?

I rode home on a bike
without underwear, imitating sex.
Something clinging with an anemic
fist to my throat.

The voices that make a person slap
her sometimes idiot head,
they might just be the mind
in its town fair stages of rot.

If I wake in Andalucia, smack inside
a farm painting, is it my responsibility
to be there while my desert home
shifts in pieces?

I had to think of him eating some produce.
I had to mishear every word, which is proof
of the two places embracing
ugliness will reach for.

How to get over this is a lecture best lost
in the push broom, the beach, a night out.
I make of myself a new relative.
I mean, I'm all over it.

Eyesore, Eggful

during K.

I

Gerbera daisies strain their heavy necks
up with green wire, wrapped around
the stems like soda straws. Living,
we have these few things: the thin cello
of each other's backs, Matisse women
with their watery reclining legs,
a simply rendered Hallelujah song
fading into applause into a rain storm.

You are a tall stick in a Flagstaff bed.
I don't touch your lips. Barking dogs
mollify the empty street.
The rest is under my dress.

II

I think your voice came from a painting,
though visually music is fruit to me,
which I said in a car in Oklahoma, also:
I'd like to be in a smoky club right now
with music about to begin and you and
a green drink on the table. I want to say
it is that simple: we survive what we want
to survive and go dead of our own volition.

Water is humming. You make space
for a spirit who comes, now less lonely.

III

I told you I could go, that was my weapon,
that and Chagall's ethereal heads, love
whispered in the ears and dancers,
harlequins, a whole village of love
in the ears and breath.

Proclaim! We run our hearts down
by the Santa Cruz river, do the bread-
and-butter where the road parts, run
alarmingly fast and stop to hear the beat
disperse in our brains like a take-off
of pigeons, like a slowing-down drum.

Crowns of water slide off our tired backs.
One biker jangles the morning solitude
in this underpass.

IV

Maybe you're locked into my soul more
than I am into yours and so what?,
asks the Amtrak in its silver,
cross-country shuffle. The best thing
I did today was wave *hellooo!*
to a train driver in my all-cotton dress.
Of Tucson, I miss the squat stucco houses
swarms of stars & the far-off echo
of a chicken-scratch violin.
You and your wily clarinet.
The way the train station smells
in the morning, the way that Mexican man
spits out the side of his mouth, or
a bird cranes its small neck
to empire a crumb of bread.

I reclaim a so-far-unorchestrated sky
then sit down to potatoes and toast.

V

I'm telling this story on the roof
to a Swedish woman in town for a chant,
while the earth grows larger and more
delicate, like the less and less resilient
innerworlds of our parents.

Dear Pendulum-sun, we ask: *who isn't a mosaic?*
Who couldn't be a masterpiece. You,
chasing moons and asteroid belts, you are the one
with a voice. We hear you like to suggest
our raucous Tucson sky as a wedding dress.

Tonight the breathing in of you is worth the rain not being here.

VI

Past the 9th street window it is a requirement
to be visibly naked behind, past the shame
of being that close to the leveling of the Central Hotel
with no mourners in sight,
I go past, my head full of bees.

I remember Mágico, a Mexican cartoon.
A Canadian sky exploding on itself
with stars, a lake of stars, lattice
of boat lights and elliptical water.

But tonight, in this part of America,
a fistful of fashion teens, new anemones
in the sea of the city which is really a town
disguised as the most lovely desert.

Walking home there are the ghostly hollyhocks,
a violence. A bar oozing beerstink, dimestore crowd
outside it across from 3 more crack houses.
An eyesore, eggful.
A man tells a woman to *quit it bitch*, and I cut
through the garden all the way back swearing
to no one I smell vegetables growing in the dark.

two

Song for a Cup and a Plate

The skeletal summer is sticking it to us,
a roaster of grand proportions egged on
by sarcastically single wet bars,
our childless, dateless dance hall thighs.

Dear open-throated summer of the all-occasion
little black dress!, each spaghetti strap an eon
marked, a mitzvah beside bored buttons
of naked cola left in glasses, blinking.

This is the season of high-heeled loafers and ruin,
occasional kisses from rainstorms, and
our sweethearts flex to love us in the anorexic dark,
forgive our still loitering torsos.

The men call it "love," though bodies of food
are policed, and the billy-club, club-footed words
they speak are teenage, brooding,
morning pears— wrong

as the *make-up-with-me* breakfasts
of women starved to believe
there's something useful to this contusion,
something expressly industrial in its design.

I Have Gone to Seek a Wife

This checklisting in The Beauty Bar
by Boy with elusive rainbow patch,
Lucky Plane Man in moody-issue boots,
these Lucite, deft, stick-and-move breathers,
thinking it's okay to hover
are really young generals besting us
with perpetual ask and rocketry,
staving off views of tiger-gripped sunsets,
bowls of clear soup in the clear lake
of evening, which itself is a vague alarm
of harp walking forward—

                    —all done in search
of the girl most unlikely to
flag or disable, so that seconds
after minking her one can leave
disguised as a jug
of purple flowers repeating,
as the lonely ingrate at her neck,
as the indiscernible tug of her
windowside petunia, for water.

Hope Is Pesky to Air

When there is no one to speak to
I am noisiest of all. I am corrected
by swallows of sunlight, squints.
I don't know my neighbors: how flawed this is.
What shall I record?
Park-goers set like gumdrops
on a lawn, the murky pond-oval,
dilapidated swans? I'm not that
excellent an historian.

Maybes, mere obstacles.
Lightposts rob the trees of some small, leafy glory.
Bulbs over-star themselves into earth.

Not Knowing

what to make of this cowboy evening—
blue-backed, famous, lording its heat

over us like a sermon, I breathe
into my knees. How can I say maybe,

that maybe you live nowhere until
the books are on the shelves,

until you leave the wide Etruscan city
on your wall, finally remember

it is ancient? I could go on musing
over amber in Vetulonia,

your thrilling terra cotta head. Your boots
made from glad leather hurt and won't

give up one minute. I'm unpolished
and unpracticed, tired of handing over

my words to stars. What can they know,
suspended like that in some blue-black

galaxy of their own? I am this far away. I don't know
where you can find me. Search the dusty rodeo in your head.

Day & Night & In Between

Trees go orange; matches
are the color of bright mud.
I miss the company of women,
their bad decisions gone over
like an airport walkway of *if only,*
the nude voice of their nude sketches
stapled shut. All their clean lines
cruise my brain like afternoon,
like the unfinished conversation
between us and whatever is next
is a tractor at the end of my street
I spy on a night of rain.

Carpooling with the Record Guy

Your vacuously silly and drunk like partial Spring,
in-my-car face is an expert pleasure to witness
one Friday evening, while two sweaters knit themselves
to sleep on your barrel-body and the party back there
continues with designer-types & thrift store lamps
& a strangely unsinister face of rock n' roll.

My laissez-faire whack of mistrust
means I don't get your silent grinny smirk
at all as contentment, don't know
what you weed out of me isn't sexual,
though the timed-out streetlights might have cooperated
vaguely in that case, the mood all moody—

I just drop you velvet-mouthed and old-man shuffling
off on the porch you have with grill and geranium
made much of. And I care about this unhaughty night
closing down, the carnival in your face at the sound
of the 7-inch release, the dedicated to-and-fro
of your platonic body which like the lightbulb flickers,
                              hey thanks, man!, and goes off.

A Boy & His Guitar

Take those orange things from your ears and reacquaint them
with my pleading voice, it's just a rock show,
another hideout for manacled regular love,

another shrill chord worshipped too late
and belly badly pierced as night with noise
that speaks for us, it's not OK with me.

So what if all the girls agreed once we turned young
to weigh the attention of cool boys against the desire
to diesel upstream ourselves, how now

to escape crouching in a party dress (*should I stay?*)
on some jerk's floor while he snores & cares less
& strums himself better to sleep?

We understand little: the hair misparted confusingly
like thighs, the emotionally unflecked face from steakhead
to steakhead being made into medium asses by cable access

& the hold on their girls, semi-automatic. A horn honk
into disobedient evening. The car radio is the bitch
that can't aniticipate your shining need. Who could?

Stop keeping that uproariously uncomplex snarl
so obviously to yourself—you alone are not the lost teen
skein of alive that joins us. Like girls we can shun

these amphibian nights, knowing not one of us
anywhere else is whispering to her instrumental lover
exactly what he believes he hears.

Superheroes

Now that he will never be alone,
the Ace-Flyer, Moustachioed Madman,
now that he is over it all,
and his skinny wife is a slab vowing
never to go awry or rotten belly-up,

finally he is ageless and unforlorn, crackling achey
& magical in the eyes of middleschool girls whose knife-tales
and lipstick shades are mighty, mighty secrets he cocks
his head to infiltrate, to hear. He in his hideout

and you with your simian haricut in a room off the highway,
you are locomotives christened—
sometimes without forgiveness

the best you can hope for is to run while the earth is thin
and the freeway crumbles to the slick black critique
of pavement your town provides.

In an older life you could sway like the guise
of a building unthoughtfully leapt and go back
to him disguised as your true self.

Saints in the Hedges

Her face at the end of this argument keeps me
well one day and a half. For the sake of
this saint, whose name is a green blur,
let me continue. Things at this height get so dizzy.

More and more I trust shoes and baseball.
Trust the kind of thinking that disregards the self
briefly. Please trust your strength is pressure asserted,
and not your image of strength, which is flawed.

Beyond this trip, clutched photo of my barefoot saint,
and echo of a cracked bat, some malaise
is bothering hope; our lives are made plain
and less sacred by the hour.

No maps show the dangerless places, just towns
which from the air you know by dizzy suns
or flawed images of saints in the hedges
strewn like pinwheels.

The Cartographer

To be in Tuscany with a bowl of olives,
not being someone else. To be in Tunisia.
In America once, I strained so closely
to the lives of others, I forgot to be
in my own. There will always be others,
with strictly buttoned coats, their own brand
of music. My father and Norman toast
once to Estonia, twice, and a third time
for all Baltic Nations. Their favorite toast.
The Tucson kitchen below the roof
which goes on saving me all night, or
the bedroom in Worcester now so unsafe
I can't sleep there. Green living room.
Embarrassing plastic plant. It's worth
staying in a place you most feel like leaving
—when a coastal wind crisscrosses
with your voice, or when each tree claims
one of your burdens as its own.
This way you dress up a tree, skirt it,
live beneath it, decidous or not.

for Stacey

Her Lucky Days

Even Jesus can't save the failed marriage
of anger to free time.

∾

The story of my piggy legs which were not so piggy,
began with an unthinkable daisy face on the commuter train.
Oatless boys I loved like mad rockets with my rainy midriff.

∾

It's thinner than I think, the gin that Disneys.
The injurious Floridian turns my fawn face brutish.

∾

I don't miss him, many pounds later.
No hollering to link us.

De Facto New Year

Pretends well-remembered boy pouring ½ & ½
in blue container might still hold her
dearly, herself needing guardrails
and compassion to ease into
next millennium, day.

Last night's tin gods and brave innuendoes
are this morning's dented heaven, barrage
of no-longer-affectionate-shadows
and the sky's Sunday: clean slate.

Daisies in mason jar refuse natural death.
She offers the bar of soap up
to the shower spray like a single egg.
Side-shadow of sand-dollar nightlight
is an angel's wing. Entire bathroom
the memory of a Mexican church. Embellished.

In Mexico in every room she wanted
one thing beautiful, she wanted proof.
In America, the comfort of owning
the right word, exact phrase,
most intelligent sentence. Truth is:
she really can't plan their final minute
together, nor capture the mysterious future
accruing every second after this one,
furious, with her name on.

Seasonal

It takes bravery and weather to arrive at a day like this.
    It isn't a globe like last time; it's a marble
lodged in some corner room or corner,
    I don't know where.
It's a light that grazes our plain hips each morning.
    It's the angry words heaved at the sky.
It is no one's fault.
    It's the mute candle, refusing to light for one decent dinner.
It is not what I mean to say: sorry.
    It's some dailiness bothering hope.
It's living between moments so the next one always shows.
    It is a matter of trust (the candle in which we take care).
These are the bodies that recover.
    Those words we hurl at the sky dismantle, and are prayer.

for Bridget

three

Summer in All Directions

For love of jargon we idle this far
between your not being able to read me
and my caring about it—

while farther east acquaintances slug
mussels for profit but eat them
anyway steamed in beer.

I can imagine the vineyard now,
see the 3 thousand for rent,
trim collarbones,

while you speak a nervous Spanish
in Hermosillo, hands implanted in dark earth
and on your knees finally.

I'll be at home with your microwave,
your 2-way grill, a life made so convenient
in your absence, dearheart,

there are Mexican vegetables dying
for a good pair of hands. *There is
the you & I you & I cannot reconcile.*

Your image here on the river
is part of the hard way things are,
floated from some upstream heavy wind.

I'm on this tiger-colored, washed-out rock
which cares less. Slipping, could I
save myself? Being honest, could I slip?

In an Embassy room south of Tepic
white curtains are the only allowable breath.

You get tired the exact moment I break silence and tell the truth.

Landscape Without Hands

There was the wake to the steady train,
a child screaming *burro, burro.*
Outside a landscape quickened
and diminished, red dust and sun.

In the light of this new country
the complicated self became history,
something well-stashed beside
the torn pants, the toothpaste.

Later in the high-walled room there was touch
but no hands, no hands, so there was collision:
the breath of the flowered curtain with your neck.
Dream made their absence starker.

The country took only our hands.

A Plane View of Home

Having no say over the emotion, I chronicle
the hours skipped and missed, behind me
ticking off in a mint-colored kitchen.

The star-splinters still shine above
the Exotic African Superette.
The rescue includes embracing
any conversation off the subject
of home, pilfered books, the view
from the railing, the hour of streetlamps.

I'll get there soon enough.
When I sleep the sky will backstitch
the day into someone else's memory.
The porthole is hanging.

Poema de Acclimación 3, España: Iggy como angula
(Acclimation Poem 3: Iggy as an eel)

I am either in this world
or the one I blink back.
Given that, I slug a book
in a bag and head for the sea,
cut right through the Barrio Xino,
trapped in the pissy smell.

Last night I was given the electric eel
muscle and fishbone flesh of Iggy Pop,
so whether or not I had a big ass
diminished in importance. I got to see
Iggy grind his tiny one all over, be a rush
of Spanish clapping hands.

It's not that you're gone, it's that
a new life has taken over, and dictates
like the Costa Brava's tiger-sea.
So if I can look out today
to the farthest point of Catalonia,
if seawater pummels weary cliffrock
and Marta's dad walks around
in his pajamas all day, I guess
I should thank myself. Seven
raincoats on a beach. Flora
greener than a fable. Hairless Iggy
reels in dreams, resides in the hips.
I'm so close to loving it.

Lineaments

Where did you go after I cursed you
across a public square in Mexico City?
I had my fears. I had forgotten
to love myself 3 cities in a row,
your face was blank or a caption.
Hotels had promised and not delivered.
The heat was a film. The stories I read
did little, did not take in my memory
or expand, and I saw true curves
in your face but ignored them.
They didn't stop me.

Sensitive subject meant I'd already decided on your response.

∾

I was glad at least for the story of oranges, grown that way
opened, found filled with diamonds.

An apple cut across and not down is the face of a star.

Subdivision, Barrio Anita

Its bottom rusted, gone speechless
so long: the separateness
that happens even as we speak,
whether I'm open or not, whether
I choose sitting by a table
of apples, or standing, as I do,
with the light of other days
around me. You appear, do not.
You appear and are voted down
by memory. You do not appear
are conjured up, atom
by iridescent atom,
your barely parted mouth
in constant flux with air
and the air specific to it,
air which is a chrisom,
chrisom which is yourself.

How incomplete you seem! Not ready
to be placed in one world or another,
this world or the next.

Obedient as ten gold buttons. Rusted horse.
Rose-colored, immaculate, kept to be untouched
as a parent's bedroom.
It's no surprise to see your hands
skim tall-stemmed grass

as though it were something
precious others trampled.

Steering the Violet Bike

These days the only terrific song coming off
your head is Spanish. You wish the dead dog

ahead would be a palm frond, the hand
above you would be your own. The commas

in the clouds jerk off to the thrill of sky and
extension of body your bike beneath you is,

your helmet atop your head a meringue
you might be married to, a job, an affair you ride to forget.

So shot up with options I rejoice
to shut down. The highway's handsome butchery

is a dance remix of the original:
a freshly splayed bluebird. What—again?

Now that I believe the burn on my cheek
I can relinquish target status and be a partner,

though I liked being the first of my friends
to marry into low self-esteem.

Contemptable freedom, is that you addicting us?
We jut out and you, oceanic, occasional pal,
give us day after day of kabillion decisions.

I stop to buy eggs and cream, tarragon and fish.
A persimmon glimmers, and I figure at best

it is flailing around to brave the porkbarrel of faces
annoyed, to settle as comfortably as we have

into the earth's unforgivable hole.

Wedding Present

The bones on honeymoon scraping each other
is what I think of, the oil-less, fatless sauces
and plates stacked like anger in his face,

but not his body, or in her ricochet tongue, but not her face.
And the ferocity with which they must not be alone,
as equal to the exquisitely wasted flesh their Stairmaster

has seen and since matched, regret a plain and blameless ceiling.
Didn't I see her once uncriminal and loosely broadcasted ass,
not resplendent! as mirrored in his face unfolding,

his seismic attention to loaded dolls? The ceremony now
assaulted by false mariachi protrudes like his one hipbone
plinking hers, a sound that bruises and weds them.

My forgiveness is a bare unbalanced egg:
His family standing bland and bastioned.
His bony bride in her tiny petal gown.

Southwestern

Attend a life and the rough gate is open, meowing.
The rifled farmer retreats. Rules fall away when, wrongly,
they'd become drum skin. There was no breathing.

Mesquite, ruin, adobe, corral: these were branded by sun
and the air going heavy past Tucson. *Animas, windmill.*
If I loved you before I stood awake, it was my own undoing.

By the kitchen it is a broken pact with God to sit in,
a saguaro offers its hundredyear arm. The mountain
is a base and a teacher, base and a lesson, hillside, command.

If a storm hides, the sheep make a bracelet and lay down.
The door hasp is a throat of wind being fantastic,
the air unsalty, phenomenal. *Chapel and junkyard. Agave.*

If my laugh had been less devotional, more steely—
If your regional face, your district—

You are geologically young.
Slacks mishung on acceptable hips
like want, their universal season.

Who Sees Us as Whole Must First Be Us

Remember your own beauty as though it were an instruction.
Remember a hornless goat found lost in the desert wild.
Runs like a dog.

Pay attention to your beery breath, your sea legs,
not how many slow and jealous miles you've logged
beside the Charles. Pray never to get the entire story.

To the taciturn face and unlarge welcome, another
TV jock concussioned into breathing your name,
or beach native's sculpted come-on:

Come on, you can't even.

Better than faking *esprit-de-corps* during dryer revolutions,
committing career suicide for one night of languid party lines,
being bride to any particular Rolling Rock, to keep this

freedom neither sloppy nor doctrinaire. Let evenings grow
bilingual, more nonplussed than neutral. After a set
of seven brights, wake to hear yourself and do not mind.

Wedding Past, Imperfect

That your goat face might have been subsumed
by fear and Christian love is obvious,
that your atomic rage became a brotherly place
where people eat small salads and stall
their language, slakeless forever,
into kitchen baskets overrun with limes
and bills and a solitude you have
vowed before God and family
to never remotely fathom.

Our actually dull kismet forsweared now,
brief and ogreish tea light, I admit I did broach myself
like a mother on the sly,
precocious side, a pre-teen kittening
and jogging her new chest
in some sordid swim routine at the Y,
misproclaiming the undereye charcoal slash
to tallyho the violence free inside you.

Where once the angel vied angelically
to hustle anger, now forgiveness—
The minutes I gave, they were supposed to be mine.

Arguing in Public

Any plastic flower's lame reach to heaven is any Dos Equis'
knowledge of terror,
so you go a few rounds of proving emphatically nothing,
grow up prickly and worn
before you've gotten a chance to rotten each other the long way.
Couples of this taquería,
I could use you being happier if you wouldn't mind it,
because the heater emits only flowers
of heat, and the birds caught in the air ducts are shrieking
like his best afternoon
of locking me out and calling the police, & the police laughing.
May you never again call each other *jerkass*
in a car on a Saturday morning,
while your love and hate deprivatize.
May your foolhearted means
of courting what is over be over now. Structureless as you are,
try thanking your respective bellies
for being potlike, the winter's weird fingers for a fury
more gracile than all your years alone.

Beautiful According to Others

You haven't begged for *no sun* this hard since Tucson,
since the awake of dream where he dissed you
got counteracted by his lawn-rabbit gift. Since then.
Since you were one of a hundred girls in a lifetime
of mimic, your voice a show-offy circus.

Leaving the familiar was all you wanted
to know: *Have I done it?*
Then where is my incremental grace?
It's a noble act the knuckled day
and birds made with their necks:
good-bye. good-bye.

Say beauty is less the spirit ungluing,
more the way you don't now punch your head.
Say you are lonely with this knowledge.
You have never felt failures
more emphatically: they're incurable.

Say you are willing to do all this
weird shifting of weight:
go back and high-five the asshole,
correct the obsessor, take the fantasy away
from itself. Say you are willing
to be misunderstood for a life like this,
with yourself as the hardest
to be with, to live through, to welcome.

about the author

Andrea Werblin has published poetry in various journals and books, as well as numerous articles on poetry. An earlier version of *Lullaby for One Fist* received an honorable mention in the Barnard New Women Series Poets Prize in 1997 (judge: Brenda Hillman).